Celebrate!
PassOver

Mike Hirst

W
HODDER
Wayland
an imprint of Hodder
Children's Books

CHINESE NEW YEAR
CHRISTMAS
DIWALI
EASTER
ID-UL-FITR

All Hodder Wayland books encourage children to read and help them improve their literacy.

✓ The contents page, page numbers, headings and index help locate specific pieces of information.

✓ The glossary reinforces alphabetic knowledge and extends vocabulary.

✓ The 'finding out more' section suggests other books, websites and organisations dealing with the same subject.

This book is based on the original title **Passover** in the *Festivals* series, published in 1997 by Wayland Publishers Ltd.

Editor: Nicola Wright
Designers: Tim Mayer and Malcolm Walker

First published in 2000 by Hodder Wayland, an imprint of Hodder Children's Books
This paperback edition published in 2002

© Copyright 2000 Hodder Wayland

A catalogue record for this book is available from the British Library

ISBN 0 7502 4045 8

Printed and bound in Hong Kong
Hodder Children's Books
a division of Hodder Headline Limited
338 Euston Road, London NW1 3BH

A note on pronunciation
In Hebrew, there is a throaty sound which sounds like the 'ch' in 'loch' or 'Bach'. In some books, it is written with the letters 'ch' but it does not sound like the 'ch' in 'chips'. In this book and some others, it is written as 'h', for example, Pesah and hametz.

A note on dates
Each religion has its own system for counting the years of its history. The starting point may be related to the birth or death of a special person or an important event. In everyday life, today, when different communities have dealings with each other, they need to use the same counting system for setting dates in the future and writing accounts of the past. The Western system is now used throughout the world. It is based on Christian beliefs about Jesus: AD (Anno Domini = in the year of our Lord) and BC (Before Christ). Members of the various world faiths use the common Western system, but, instead of AD and BC, they say and write CE (in the Common Era) and BCE (before the Common Era).

Cover picture: Two young Jewish boys taking part in the Pesah supper customs.

Picture acknowledgements:
Commissioned photography by Alain Attar of The Agency for Jewish Education *cover*, Guy Hall 12 (top), 22, 23 (both), 25 (bottom) and Rupert Horrox *title page*, 5, 17, 18, 19, 20, 21, 24, 26; Photri 7; Zev Radovan 11 (bottom), 12 (bottom), 13, 15 (both), 17 (bottom), 25 (top), 27, 28; Trip 10 (Helen Rogers), 16 (bottom) (E James); Angela Wood 8, 9, 11 (top), 14 (both), 29 (both); Zefa 16 (top).

The photograph on page 10 is by Mr Heinz Seelig, published by Palphot, Herzlia, Israel.
The photograph on page 21 was published in 'Diaspora Haggadah' by Yanin Enterprises, Israel in 1988.

Contents

Words that appear in **bold** in the text are explained in the Glossary on page 30.

Jews Around the World

These countries helped Jews during the Holocaust.

SCANDINAVIA

RUSSIA (FORMER SOVIET UNION)

Jews have lived here for 1,500 years. In recent times, many Russian Jews have moved to the USA and Israel.

Many Jews lived here until the 1930s. The German leader, Adolf Hitler attacked the Jews in the 1930s and 40s. Many Jews fled. Jews who stayed behind were murdered by Hitler and his Nazis. This terrible time in Jewish history is called the Holocaust.

EASTERN EUROPE

PORTUGAL SPAIN

Jews lived here in the Middle Ages, until the Christian rulers made them leave.

ISRAEL

NORTH AFRICA

Jews lived here for 2,000 years, but after 1948 many moved to Israel.

CHINA

INDIA

ETHIOPIA

Jews lived here for over 2,000 years. Since 1948, most have left to live in Israel or English-speaking countries.

Jews lived here for 3,000 years, but in the 1980s they were badly treated. Most went to Israel.

Jews lived here in ancient times. In 1948, Israel became a Jewish country again. Many Jews live there today.

AUSTRALIA

SOUTH AFRICA

A small number of Jews escaped the Holocaust and settled here.

4

The first Jews lived in the Middle East over 3,000 years ago. Their home was in the land of Israel.

After the year 70 CE, many Jews went to live in other parts of the world. This map shows countries where Jews have lived.

▲ All over the world, Jewish families enjoy the festival of Passover.

USA

Jews have gone to live in the USA since the 1700s. Today, more than a third of all Jews live in the USA.

About 30,000 Jews escaped the Holocaust and settled in China, especially in Shanghai.

Some Jews who escaped the Holocaust went to live in Australia.

Countries in South America let some Jews in during the Holocaust.

SOUTH AMERICA

We Want to be Free

Passover is the most important Jewish festival. It happens once a year, in March or April.

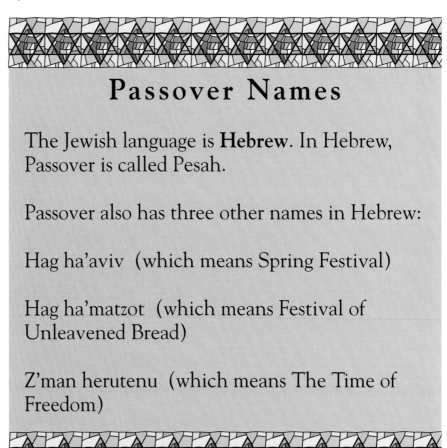

Passover Names

The Jewish language is **Hebrew**. In Hebrew, Passover is called Pesah.

Passover also has three other names in Hebrew:

Hag ha'aviv (which means Spring Festival)

Hag ha'matzot (which means Festival of Unleavened Bread)

Z'man herutenu (which means The Time of Freedom)

Passover is a time when Jews remember an important story from their history. About 3,000 years ago, the Jewish people lived in Egypt. They were slaves. A great leader called Moshe, or Moses, was born. With God's help, he led the Jews to freedom in a new land.

▶ At Pesah Jewish families eat a special meal called the **seder**.

Moshe, the Great Leader

The ruler of Egypt was the **pharaoh**. He made his Jewish slaves work very hard. He even ordered his soldiers to kill all the Jewish baby boys. But one Jewish woman saved her baby. She hid him in a basket by the river. The baby was called Moshe.

◄ This picture shows slaves being forced to work in Egypt.

► A painting of Moshe and the burning bush.

Pharaoh's daughter found baby Moshe. She took him home and looked after him. Later, when he had grown up, Moshe realized how wicked the pharaoh was. He ran away and went to work for a shepherd in the desert.

One day, Moshe saw a burning bush. God spoke to Moshe out of the flames. He told Moshe to go back to Egypt and set free the Jewish slaves.

Escape from Egypt

At first, pharaoh did not want to set free his Jewish slaves. So God sent ten horrible **plagues** into Egypt.

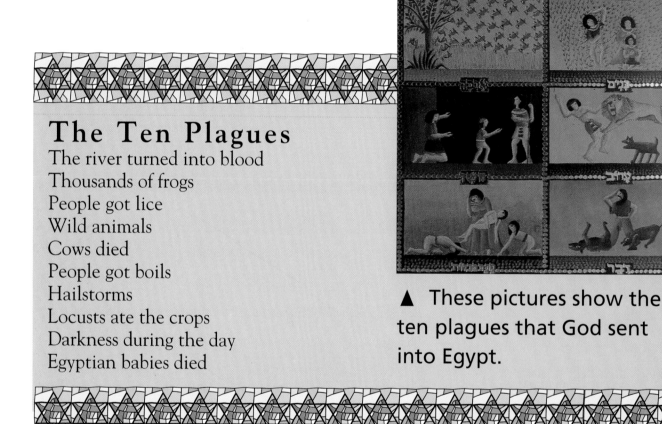

The Ten Plagues
The river turned into blood
Thousands of frogs
People got lice
Wild animals
Cows died
People got boils
Hailstorms
Locusts ate the crops
Darkness during the day
Egyptian babies died

▲ These pictures show the ten plagues that God sent into Egypt.

Each plague brought terrible suffering to the Egyptian people. At last, pharaoh said that the Jews could leave.

► This painting shows the Sea of Reeds and the drowned Egyptian soldiers and their horses. Today the Sea of Reeds is called the Red Sea.

Moshe led the Jewish people to the Sea of Reeds. Suddenly, pharaoh changed his mind again and sent soldiers to stop the Jews leaving Egypt. Now God showed Moshe a way across the sea on dry land. The soldiers followed the Jews, but the waters rose and they were drowned.

► This old painting shows the Jewish women singing and dancing. They are celebrating because they have escaped from Egypt.

Food for Pesah

When the Jewish slaves left Egypt, they had to hurry. They made bread, but had no time to let the dough rise. They put the dough straight in the oven, and it came out flat. This flat bread is called **unleavened bread**, or **matzah**.

▲ Many foods have special ingredients to make them light and fluffy. In Hebrew, these ingredients are called **hametz**. At Pesah, Jews try to eat food without any hametz in it.

Today, Jews eat unleavened bread at Pesah.

► These young people are making unleavened bread. In Hebrew, this bread is called matzah.

◄ A baker putting matzah in the oven.

So that the dough does not rise on its own, the bakers have only a few minutes to make and bake matzah.

There are two main groups of Jewish people.

Ashkenazi Jews lived in the north of Europe and North America.

Sephardi Jews lived in the south of Europe and the Middle East.

These two groups sometimes eat different kinds of food at Pesah, but all Jews eat matzah.

Getting Ready for Pesah

Before the start of Pesah, Jewish families spring-clean their houses.

Pesah lasts for one week. During that time, nobody should eat any food with hametz in it. Jewish families clean their homes to make sure there is no hametz left in the house.

Children sometimes play a game called Hunt the Hametz. An adult hides small pieces of hametz food around the home. Then they turn down the lights.

The children have a candle, a feather and a paper bag. They set off to find the hametz food. When they find the food, they scoop it into the bag with the feather.

▲ Playing Hunt the Hametz.

◄ This girl is putting old hametz food onto the fire.

► In Jerusalem, many families burn old hametz food on one big bonfire.

On the morning before Pesah, Jews make a fire. Before the festival begins, they burn any old food with hametz in it.

► The men are cleaning pots and dishes ready for Pesah.

15

The Pesah Supper

On the first day of Pesah, the family meets in the evening. They eat a special meal called the seder.

The seder usually lasts for three to six hours. People sing and tell stories as well as eating.

The seder has fourteen parts to it. One person leads the seder to make sure the parts happen in the right order.

▲ In this family, the leader of the seder wears a white gown.

1 Kiddush
Jews say or sing a prayer called a blessing.

2 Washing the hands
The leader of the seder washes their hands.

◄ This Jewish woman is using a special jug and bowl to wash her hands.

3 Karpas
Everyone eats a piece of vegetable dipped in salty water or vinegar.

4 Dividing the matzah
The leader breaks a piece of matzah. Then the leader hides one half of the broken matzah, called the **afikomen**.

5 The story
The family hears the story of Pesah.

6 Washing the hands
The leader of the seder washes their hands again.

▲ The leader of the seder breaks a piece of matzah in two.

► Can you see a book next to the matzah? This book is a **haggadah** and it tells the Pesah story.

7 Blessing the matzah

The leader blesses the matzah and gives everyone a piece to eat.

8 The bitter vegetable

Everybody eats a piece of bitter vegetable. The nasty taste reminds them that the Jews were once slaves.

9 Sandwich

This is another piece of bitter vegetable eaten between two pieces of matzah.

10 The meal

Everyone eats the rest of the Pesah food. At the end of the meal, children go off to find the hidden afikomen.

► The bitter vegetable may be a horseradish or the inside of a lettuce.

11 Finding the hidden matzah

When someone finds the afikomen, the leader shares it with the rest of the family.

12 Thanks for the meal

People say poems and sing songs to thank God for the Pesah food.

13 Praise

There are songs about how good it is to be free.

14 The seder ends

▲ In many families, the child who finds the afikomen wins a prize.

Remembering the Past

Before Pesah, a child in the family learns four questions in Hebrew. The questions ask why Pesah is a special time of year.

When the family gets together for the seder, the child says or sings the four questions they have learned.

The Jewish holy book is called the **Torah**. The Torah says that God helped the Jewish slaves in four ways. During the seder everyone has four drinks of wine or grape juice, to remind them of how good God is.

▼ Parents feel proud when their child remembers the four questions.

Pesah Song

Jews sing special songs
at Pesah.

One song explains why Pesah
is different from any other time
of year.

At Pesah we eat matzah for
our bread.
At Pesah we eat bitter foods to
remind us of the slaves.
At Pesah we remember the
tears of the slaves.
At Pesah we remember that
today we are free.

▲ Jews believe that people should
read the holy books carefully, to learn
about the past. In this picture, a wise
man is reading thoughtfully. The foolish
people are playing in a tree, doing
handstands and stamping angrily.

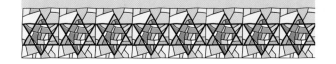

Food Customs

During the seder, some of the foods have a special meaning.

Bitter foods

At the beginning of the meal, everyone eats **karpas**. Karpas is a vegetable, maybe a potato or a piece of parsley. Jews dip the karpas in salty water. The salty water reminds them of the tears and sweat of the Jewish slaves.

Later in the meal, everyone eats the bitter vegetable, called **maror**. The bitterness stands for the sadness of the slaves. However, the Pesah story has a happy ending, so Jews eat the bitter vegetable with a sweet called **haroset**.

◄ For karpas, this girl has dipped parsley in salty water.

The leader of the seder reads out the ten plagues that God sent to Egypt. For each plague, everyone dips their finger in wine, and flicks it onto a plate.

When they flick the wine, Jews remember the suffering of the Egyptian people.

▲ This girl is flicking wine.

◄ Haroset is a sweet made with apples, nuts and honey or dates.

Watching and Waiting

In Jewish history, a man called Elijah was an important leader. He was a **prophet**, just like Moshe. He gave messages from God to the ancient Jews.

When he was very old, Elijah did not die. Instead, a chariot of fire carried him up to heaven.

Jews have a legend that one day Elijah will come back to earth. He will tell the Jews about a new leader called the Messiah.

► These boys have opened the door to look for Elijah.

Every seder has an empty cup, in the middle of the table. Someone fills the cup with wine, just in case Elijah comes back to earth and visits the family.

At the end of the seder, the family also opens the door so that Elijah feels welcome if he comes.

▲ Many families have a special cup for Elijah.

◄ At the end of the evening, some children start to fall asleep.

A Holiday Week

The days at the start and end of Pesah are days for rest and worship. Besides the family seder, Jews go to a **synagogue** and read the Torah.

One special reading for Pesah comes from the Song of Songs. This is a love poem, and it reminds Jews of God's love for them.

▲ A beautiful picture from a book of the Song of Songs.

In the middle of the Pesah week, many Jews take a holiday. Jewish schools are closed, and adults take the week off work if they can.

Jews from North Africa have a special festival the day after Pesah. It is called maimuna. For maimuna, there are fairs, picnics and street parties.

▼ Many people are enjoying picnics and barbecues at this maimuna festival.

Jewish Festivals Around the Year

Rosh Hashanah

Rosh Hashanah is the New Year Festival. It happens in September or October.

▼ A horn is blown to tell everyone that the new year is beginning. At the end of Yom Kippur, the horn is blown again. It tells people that the fast is over.

Yom Kippur

At the same time as Rosh Hashanah, Jews celebrate Yom Kippur. This is the day when Jewish people say they are sorry for anything they have done wrong. On Yom Kippur, Jews have a fast. They go without eating for a whole day.

Sukkot

Sukkot happens five days after Yom Kippur. When the Jewish slaves escaped from Egypt, they did not go straight to their new home in Israel. First they lived in the desert for forty years. At Sukkot, Jews remember the time in the desert. Many people build huts or tents out of doors, and live in them for eight days.

Simhat Torah

At the end of Sukkot comes the festival of Simhat Torah. The Torah scrolls are paraded in the synagogue to celebrate the reading of the whole Torah which has taken all year.

▲ At the end of Sukkot, Jews parade the Torah in the synagogue. They walk around, holding it up high.

Shavuot

Shavuot takes place in May or June. Jews remember the time when God gave the Torah to Moshe. The Torah is the Jewish holy book.

◄ This woman is helping to decorate the place where her family will live at Sukkot.

Glossary

Afikomen Half of the matzah that is broken in two during the seder meal.

Ashkenazi Jews A group of Jewish people. Most Ashkenazi Jews have families that come from the northern parts of Europe.

Haggadah A book that tells the story of Pesah.

Hametz The ingredient in food that makes it light and fluffy. Yeast is the kind of hametz that makes bread rise.

Hebrew The Jewish language. Hebrew is the main language in Israel.

Haroset A sweet eaten during the seder meal. It is often made from apples, nuts and honey or dates.

Karpas Any bitter-tasting vegetable dipped in saltwater and eaten during the seder.

Matzah Unleavened bread. The bread looks flat, like a biscuit or a pancake, because it has no hametz in it.

Maror A bitter-tasting vegetable.

Pharaoh The leader in ancient Egypt. Pharaohs were very powerful men.

Plague A nasty event, which harms many people. An illness that kills many people is called a plague.

Prophet A person who gives messages from God to other people.

Seder The special meal that Jews eat at Pesah.

Sephardi Jews A group of Jewish people. Most Sephardi Jews have families that came from the southern part of Europe.

Synagogue A holy building, where Jews meet for prayers and religious services.

Torah The Jewish holy book. God first gave the Torah to Moshe.

Unleavened bread A kind of flat bread without hametz. In Hebrew, unleavened bread is called matzah.

Finding Out More

BOOKS TO READ

Celebrate Jewish Festivals by Angela Wood
(Heinemann, 1995)

Discovering Religions: Judaism (Heineman, 1995)

I am a Jew by Clive Lawton (Watts, 1995)

Introducing Religions: Judaism by Sue Penney
(Heineman, 1997)

Judaism by Monica Stoppleman (Watts, 1996)

Judaism by Angela Wood (Wayland, 1995)

My Jewish Life by Anne Clarke (Wayland, 1996)

Religions by Anita Ganeri (Marshall Editions, 1998)

The Kingfisher Book of Religions by Trevor Barnes
(Kingfisher, 1999)

What Do We Know About Judaism? by Doreen Fine
(Macdonald, 1996)

World of Festivals: Passover by David and Gill Rose
(Evans, 1997)

CD-ROMS

Aspects of Religion (Granada, 1999)

Exploring World Religions (Granada, 1999)

USEFUL ADDRESSES

To find out more about Judaism, you may find these
addresses useful:

Board of Deputies of British Jews,
Commonwealth House,
1–19 New Oxford Street,
London WC1A 1NF
Tel: 0171 543 5400

Jewish Music Distribution,
P.O. Box 2268,
Hendon, London NW4 3UW
Tel: 0181 203 8046

Manor House Books,
Sternberg Centre,
80 East End Road,
Finchley, London N3 2SY
Tel: 0181 346 2288

Memorial Council Bookshop,
25 Enford Street,
London W1H 1DL
Tel: 0171 724 7778

The Festival Shop,
56 Poplar Road, Kings Heath,
Birmingham BI4 7AG
Tel: 0121 444 0444

Index